P9-ASM-143

PERU
AND THE INCA
CIVILIZATION

TEXT: **M. WIESENTHAL**

Rights of total or partial reproduction and translation
reserved.
World copyright of this edition:
© GEOCOLOR,® S.A.
Travesera de Gracia, 15 - Barcelona (21) - Spain

1st. Edition, July 1978
I.S.B.N.
84-7424-015-8

Library of Congress Catalog Card Number: 78-63021
All rights reserved.
This edition is published by Crescent Books, a division of
Crown Publishers, Inc.

a   b   c   d   e   f   g   h

CRESCENT BOOKS

New York

San Martin Square, with the monument to the Argentine general sculpted by Mariano Benlliure.

HISTORY AND LEGEND

The land of Peru is the product of myth and legend. To the traveller it looks like the foam and craters of an ancient cosmic creation. It is the product of volcanoes, water, earth and cloud, of the desert and the jungle. Science itself has not yet been able to reveal the mysteries of its beginning. No one knows how its mountains and its sanctuaries were made. The Golden Bird, legend says, communicated to men the secret of changing stones into mud.

Let us listen to the poet who tells of Peru the sacred, progeny of the sun and of its shining birds, gift of the tropics, of the coca plant and paradise. Let us listen

too, to the historians who tell of a country born out of human effort and the will of its inhabitants. Perhaps this is one of the marvellous secrets of Peru's history: the modesty with which its people have concealed the bitterness of the struggle, only to show us the beauty of its fruits. Old countries have some of the magic qualities of the troubador; they enjoy transforming what was work into a miracle, and history into legend. This miraculous Peru is at the same time one of the most developed lands in South America. It had a university in 1551, railways in 1850, oil wells in 1863, and telegraphic communications in 1872. Since the far off times of its first cultures, it has witnessed the passing of the Inca empire and the Spanish rule and a long period of history and legend that ended in 1821 and 1824 with the wars and declaration of independence. Those who prefer to follow the steps of history nearer to the earth, will find great archaeological treasures in Peru. The first pre-Inca civilizations, going back several millennia, have left notable traces in the cultures of Chavín, Tiahuanaco, Nazca and Mochica.

From the XII century, the Incas made their appearance on the historical panorama of Peru. These were the last offspring of the ancient cultures of Tiahuanaco. Excellent engineers, they developed their construction techniques against a hostile nature. They built irrigation channels in the desert, mastered the technique of alloying metals, and were excellent farmers. The arrival of the Spaniards in the XVI century put an end to this powerful empire. With a small group of men, Francisco Pizarro conquered the domain of the Inca. It is quite probable that those Spanish adventurers, who had the virtues and the vices characteristic of men of action, did no more than bear witness to the crumbling of an empire weakened by internal dissention, and a mistaken administration.

The Viceroyalty of Peru stretched over the greater part of South America, until July 28th 1821, when the country's independence was proclaimed by José de San Martín, to be confirmed three years later by Bolivar in the battles of Junín and Ayacucho. The first years of the Republic were, like the first years of the Spanish conquest, anarchic and difficult. The war with Chile in 1879 complicated things further. The later years of the century, however, brought a favourable historical change. It could be said that from that time on, the country faced the new challenge of its future; important economic and social reforms today occupy the energies of the population of Peru. At present, these problems are difficult obstacles in the way of work relations. In

From top to bottom; the Municipal building of Lima;
the changing of the quard at Government Palace; and
the church of La Merced, the oldest in Lima.

A view of the large Plaza de Armas in Lima.

time they will merely be part of the miracle, legend,
and poetry of rich Peru.

LIMA

Lima is the capital of the country; it is a gay coastal
city, bustling and coquettish like its women folk. Its
name is that of a fruit and its personality distinctly
feminine. She hides her appearance behind a screen,
and takes us, on tiny feet, through the enchanting
corners of her gardens.

From the bridge to the Alameda,
She goes on tiny feet...

The old Stone Bridge built by a XVII century Viceroy
spans both banks of the Rímac. On the right is the
''bajo el Puente'', the typical old quarter of the city, a
magic labyrinth of parks, fountains, statues and con-
vents. During the viceregal period it was one of
Lima's most elegant districts. It is said that the
Viceroy Amat had the Paseo de Aguas built for a
lady — la Perricholi. But the old quarter, like all

romantic souvenirs has suffered from the passing of time. La Alameda, la Quinta de Presa —now the Viceregal Museum—, the Convent of Los Descalzos, the Acho bull ring, guard the nostalgia of Lima's past.

Nevertheless, the city has grown beyond the Bridge, towards the coast and the sea. New residential areas, San Isidro, Miraflores, Barranco, have grown up on the shore, sheltered by Lima's old spas. Through these streets, with long and noisy strides, marches the life of today: commercial activity, banks, shows, art galleries. Surfing is practised on its

Monument to Pizarro.
The cathedral of Lima.
Cloister of Santo Domingo.
House of Oquendo in the street of «El Correo».

The interior of the church of San Pedro consecrated in 1638.

The convent of San Francisco with its fine façade
and ornamented interior is one of the most impressive
buildings in Lima.

 *Three views of the Palace de Torre Tagle,
a classic monument of Lima colonial style architecture.*

beaches. A new city is developing and growing among
the gay bougainvillia of Miraflores, and the patriar-
chal olive trees of San Isidro. The city overlooks the
sea, and a long rosary of beaches at Costa Verde,
Chorrillos and La Herradura...

Pizarro's ancient capital, —which was called the City
of the Kings by the Spaniards— is still the heart of
Lima. All the history of the city is united in the Plaza
de Armas, around the lovely bronze fountain that
points out the water hours of eternity. It was here
where General San Martín proclaimed the independence of Peru in 1821. Some of the finest buildings
in Lima stand around the Plaza de Armas: the Cathedral, the Government Palace, the Casa del Oidor...
The traveller can organize his visit to the city very
easily from here. As we walk through the city there is
an infinity, or almost, of details which will detain our
steps as the day wears on, such as the water in the
fountain or the sounds in the park where we stayed
to meditate: silent and light, fugitive and fleet. Dates,

names, artistic styles, disappear very soon from the human mind. We shall visit the tomb of Pizarro in the Cathedral, the courtyard and corridor of the Torre Tagle palace, the colonial architecture of San Francisco, the baroque altars and treasure of La Merced, San Pedro and San Agustín. Perhaps we have read in a book that the Casa de la Riva and the Casona de Oquendo were built in the XVIII century. Someone has told us too, the sweet story of Isabel Flores de Oliva, Saint Rose of Lima who lived, like the birds of the air, on remnants of love. Numbers, the names of goldsmiths, erudite details, everything passes with time. And only the remains of love stay. This image of Lima with its name of a fruit and distinctly feminine personality, is like a rose caught in a plait or put in a lapel. Whoever wishes to go deeper with philological curiosity, into the secrets of Lima, can direct his steps to any of its many museums.

Interior view of the convent of San Francisco.

LIMA'S MUSEUMS

The Art Museum, inaugurated in 1956 , was built according to plans by the French engineer Gustave Eiffel. Today it contains more than 10,000 exhibits representing the whole history of Peru: primitive pottery, pictures and objets d'art from the vice regal period, furniture and pictures from the time of the Republic. In the National Anthropological and Archaeological Museum there is some ancient fabric from Paracas and a valuable collection of jewels and gold objects. The Gold Museum comprises three different collections: the extremely rich collection of gold objects and jewels; the collection of ancient weapons and a collection of precolumbine farming, hunting and fishing weapons and implements.

Among the most outstanding pieces in the museum are ornaments, statuettes and tumis — ceremonial knives belonging to the primitive cultures of the country. Precolombine pottery and fabric can also be seen in the Amano museum and in the Rafael Larco Herrera museum; objects from the viceregal period are in the Viceroyalty Museum in the Quinta de la Presa; souvenirs from the struggle for independence are on show in the National History Museum; and those fond of bull-fighting can visit the fabulous collection of capes, trophies, swords, pictures and posters in the Museo Taurino.

Two corners of modern Lima: the Statue of the Llamas, and the Monument to the Farm Worker, in the Paseo de la República.

Fabric found in the Paracas Peninsular probably dating from the first centuries of the first pre-christian millennium

A gold ceremonial knife ("tumi"), encrusted with sodalite kept in the National Anthropology and Archaeology Museum.

Pottery belonging to different cultures of Peru.

Several pieces from the Art Museum. This Museum has a notable collection of prehispanic pottery from the ancient Peruvian cultures.

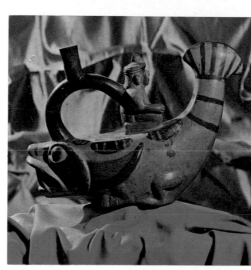

The Tello Obelisk. National Anthropological and Archeological Museum.

The swearing of Peruvian Independence (1821);
a painting kept in the Lima National History Museum.

La Mazamorra morada is the most popular dessert. It is made with cooked maize, sugar, cloves, fruit, lemon juice and cinnamon.

Creole cuisine can be accompanied with the excellent Ica wines. But there exist other more popular drinks made from maize: la chicha morada, without alcohol, and la chicha de jora which is stronger. In the river oasis of Ica they distill pisco, an extremely strong spirit.

In the restaurants of Lima almost all the dishes of creole cookery can be sampled. But on the subject of food in Lima the classic "chifas" must be mentioned. These are restaurants that serve eastern cookery, influenced by creole dishes. Fruit from the jungle gives any Peruvian meal its finishing touch of refined taste and exotic colour.

LIFE IN LIMA

Anyone who would like to contemplate life in Lima, has only to sit for a while in a cafe under the arcades in the Plaza San Martín; there he will see the passers by and try to construe their biography. Black men, white, Japanese, mulattoes, (offspring of white and black parents), zambos (from Indian and negro parents), mestizos, indians, cholos... In the streets of Lima there is an intermingling of races, of styles and periods of history, stretching from the distant past to the future. Lima is an international city with good communications to the rest of America and the rest of the world. The Panamerican Highway, converted into a many-laned motor way crosses it from north to south. The highway and the central railway link

Monument to Simón Bolívar by Tadolini, standing in the Inquisition Square.

the city with the interior crossing the Andes. The Jorge Chavez International airport and the port of Callao take care of almost all tourist and commercial activity.

THE OUTSKIRTS OF LIMA

There are many varied and interesting excursions to be enjoyed outside Lima. The scenery of the neighbouring valleys being enhanced by an ideal climate above 600 metres, and some localities of historical interest. Going along the lower valley of the Rímac, we reach Puruchuco, where there are the restored ruins of a palace that must have belonged to some petty king during the precolombine era. Via the South Panamerican Highway we reach Pachacamac, the most famous sanctuary on the central coast of Peru before the arrival of the Spaniards. Leaving Lima via the North Panamerican Highway, we cross the picturesque valleys of the rivers Chillón and Chancay surrounding the town of Ancón, the main summer resort on the sandy coastline. Enthusiasts of water sports congregate in the calm vaters of Ancón and in other lovely spots along the edge of the bay.

THE CITIES

Cities, perhaps by association, are usually similar to their inhabitants. The towns in Peru reflect the character of their people: busy and dynamic on the coast, lordly and stern in the mountains, sad and introverted in the jungle.

The night-time illuminations emphasize the beauty of the Miraflores residential area.

Two scenes from the typical dance of "Alcatraz"

The city of Lima has many fine parks.

In the Avenida del Rosario de San Isidro the "huaca de Huallamarca" or "Pan de Azúcar (sugar loaf) can be seen —an ancient temple made from sun-dried brick.

The modern auditorium in the Salazar Park and the Bridge of Sighs in Barranco.

AYACUCHO

Ayacucho is one of the towns which has kept its colonial past most intact. In the Pampa de Quinua, near to this town, the battle of Ayacucho was fought on December 9th 1824 which put an end to Spanish rule.

ICA AND NAZCA

Those who are interested in the cultural remains of the pre-Inca period would do well to go to Ica and

Nazca. Both cities are well communicated to Lima via the South Panamerican Highway. The Regional Museum at Ica houses many objects from the primitive Peruvian cultures: mummies, war trophies, pottery, cloth and gold ornaments.

In the stony areas surrounding the city of Nazca some mysterious drawings have appeared whose meaning has still not been discovered. No less interesting are the subterranean irrigation channels built by the former inhabitants of the region. These channels or "Nazca lines" run along the ground in the desert over a surface area of more than five hundred square metres. Some authors have imagined the Nazca drawings to be the outline of a landing

The Municipal Park in Barranco.

Several samples of the rich Peruvian handicrafts.

The Acho bull ring built by the Viceroy Amat.

ground for extra-terrestrial space ships. Others
interested in the subject affirm that the villages in
the region had, in the far distant past, succeeded
in flying through the air in balloons. Whatever the
origin of these Nazca lines is, the Incas did not allow
any information on them to reach us.

The Incas, being practical engineers, despised the
Nazca culture, but it is evident that this sentiment is
not shared by modern man.

CUZCO

The city of Cuzco is the archaeological capital of
Peru. Like the Andes, it has a rugged stone outline.
The highlands of Cuzco washed by the river Vilcanota stretch through a hilly jungle area on the
threshold of the Amazon. The word Cuzco (Cusco) in
Quechua means "navel". And Cuzco really is the
navel or heart of South America, the centre of the
great Inca civilization.

The city was founded around the year 1200, but its
era of splendour was in the first half of the XV
century when Pachacutec reigned over the Incas.
When the Spaniards conquered the city in 1533,
they took up residence in the old palaces. Thus in
Cuzco two great cultures were founded which were
to form the spirit of modern Peru. The Inca Garcilaso
was a mestizo from Cuzco, and from that mixture of
races and traditions there arose the most important
schools of art in the country and the ancient University of San Antonio Abad. Around the impressive
historic walls of Cuzco the traveller will find the most
impressive monuments representing this merging of
cultures: an imposing architecture with high walls
and deep foundations created with tremours from
volcanoes at the beginning of time. The Lord of the
Earth Tremours, the patron of Cuzco, is worshipped
in the cathedral. The spirit of the earth tremours has
inspired the artists who created the great archi-
tectural wonders of the city: the baroque facade of

The «chandelier» pattern on the slopes of Paracas.

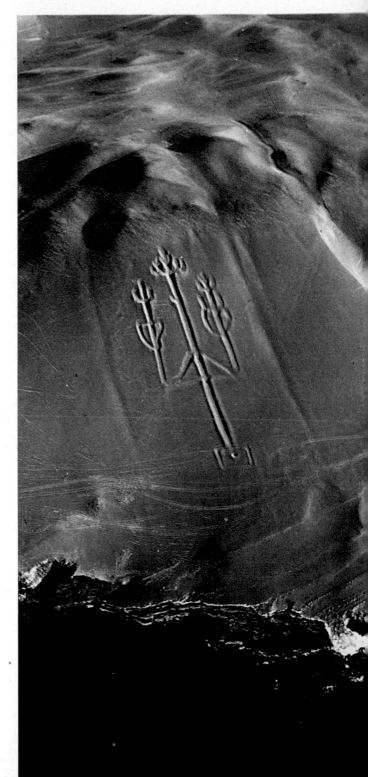

The mysterious drawings of the pampas of Nazca make one think that the ancient Peruvians knew of the technique of flight. The Englishmen Julian Nott and Jim Woodman reconstructed one of these primitive crafts to fly over the Nazca findings.

Two views of the Plaza de Armas at Cuzco with the noble façades of La Compañia and the Cathedral.

The baroque retrochoir in the Cathedral.

The pulpit of San Blas, a magnificent XVII century work of art.

the Church of the Company, the bell tower of St. Domingo —built on the temple of the sun—, the cloister of La Merced, the San Francisco lectern, the paintings of Chihuantito at Chinchero, the pulpit of San Blas, the statue of St. Sebastian carved by Melchor Huamán Mayta for the church of the same name, the statue of St. Jerome by Tomás Tuyro Túpa made for the parish of St. Anne, the paintings of Ugarte and Sinchi Roca Inca...

Colonial Cuzco was a prodigy of urban development. The Plaza de Armas still preserves its majestic dimensions and symbolizes Cuzco's lordly genealogy. At the time of the Viceroyalty it was the scene of splendid festivities with gentlemen, clerics and bishops; great personages, who, if we are to believe the popular refrain, were not always eager to pay their debts. This humorous verse is often recited throughout Peru:

The church of Santo Domingo was built on the Temple of the Sun. In the interior the remains of the Inca sanctuary can still be seen built with blocks of granite.

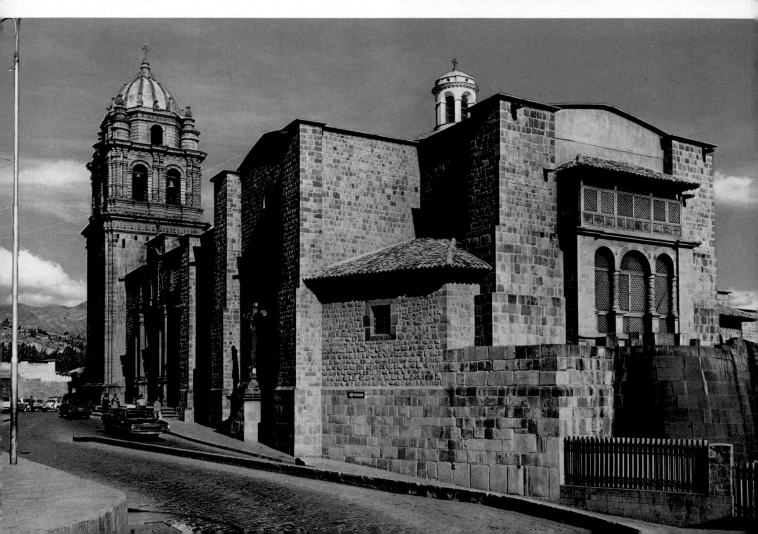

The façade and courtyard of the old Archbishop's Palace, now the Museum of Religious Art.

Valley of the Incas. In this region lie the most priceless treasures of Peruvian archaeology. Sacsayhuamán, Ollantaytambo, Machu Picchu and Pisac. And even nearer to the capital are historical places of note: Puca Pucara, the Red Fort, the fountains of Tambo Machay, and the sanctuary of Kenko, with its maze.

CAJAMARCA

In the Mountains to the north, in the middle of soft undulating countryside is Cajamarca, the historic city where Atahualpa, the last Inca king died. Its temples and portals of hewn stone give it a solemn air. The city is rich in meat and dairy products with cattle, and fruit from the rich earth. Near to the town are the thermal waters of the Inca baths where the Inca king Atahualpa was bathing when he was arrested by Pizarro's henchmen.

Inside the city, the so-called Ransom Room can still be visited; it is a thick walled chamber which, according to tradition, was twice filled with silver, and once with gold to pay the ransom for the imprisoned Inca.

TRUJILLO AND THE RUINS OF CHAN-CHAN

The city of Trujillo is of interest to the tourist in its proximity to the ruins of Chan-Chan and in the interesting documents relating to its colonial past. This was one of the largest sun-dried brick cities in the world. Its remains still bear witness to the rich culture which died out before the arrival of the Incas. Trujillo is situated in the fertile valley of Santa Catalina in an oasis bathed by the waters of the river Moche. It has some magnificent mansions and several baroque churches belonging to the Spanish period. A city of balconies and iron grilles, it is welcoming and hospitable with a pleasant transparency in its atmosphere.

The cyclopean construction of the Incas gives a characteristic look to the small streets of Cuzco.

In the house of the Inca Garcilaso de la Vega the Regional Historical Museum of Cuzco has been installed where some masterpieces of colonial art are kept.

An enormous wall of Inca masonry lines the Callejón de Loreto.

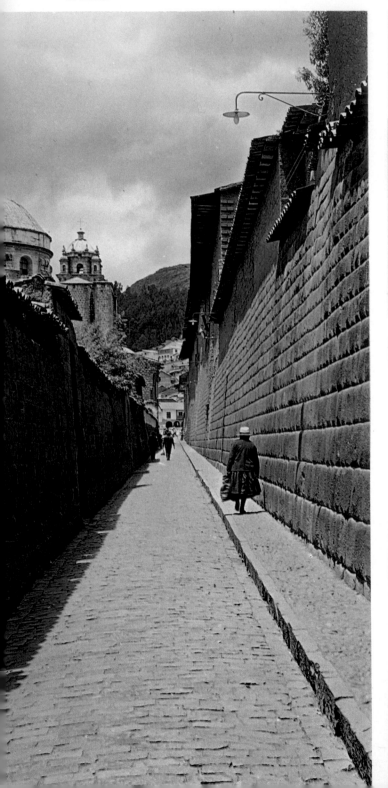

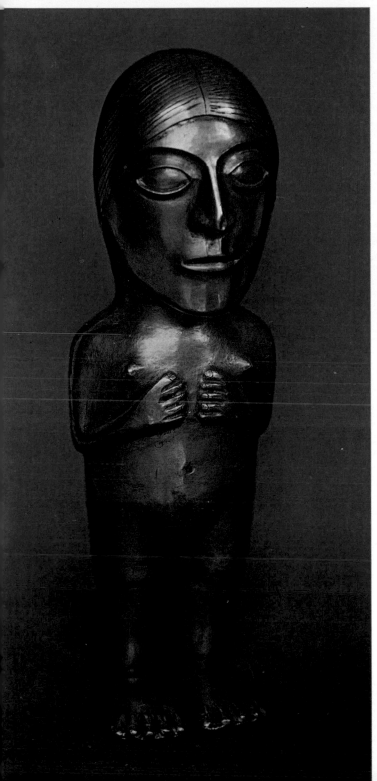

Proceeding along the left bank of the river Moche via the dusty paths through estates and fields, we reach the Pampa de los Mochicas. Two gigantic monuments in sun-dried brick —la Huaca of the sun and la Huaca of the moon— have survived from the ancient Mochica civilization, masters in irrigation and in the utilization of river water.

CRAFTS

In the lesser arts, the spirit of the indian has pre-

Pottery and gold objects from the Inca cultures found in the Cuzco region.

37

vailed from the colonial period onwards. Even in Peru's greatest monuments the indigenous talent for decoration is constantly evident in altar-pieces, carvings, ornaments, and gold jewellery.

The city of Ayacucho created a type of art which, in modern times, has gained great popularity on the tourist market. They are the famous San Marcos wood and alabaster altar-pieces depicting religious scenes. But let us not forget that the primitive Peruvian cultures were also rich in other crafts:- weaving, pottery, and metal work. Using the wool spun by the women on their spinning wheels, the native weaver has created beautiful samples of cloth, still dyed according to the pre-Inca methods. The pottery tradition cultivated by the ancient Nazcas and Mochicas is still carried on by popular craftsmen. Some fine examples of this craft are the beetles from Pucará.

The aesthetic sense of the Peruvian people finds expression in the whole sphere of peasant life: in the

baskets, straw hats, the horses and mules' harnesses, in the painted clay pottery and the pyrographed gourds, known as sculpted mate in Perú. Many religious objects such as candles and crucifixes, have also been transformed into works of art by the miracle of the indian genius. It is a worth while experience to contemplate these lovely objects in the colourful atmosphere of fiestas and pilgrimages. The Peruvian soul is an interesting mixture of spirituality and superstition, fervour and sceptical satire, melancholy and joy.

THE FOLKLORE

There is also a rich mixture of cultures, traditions and

A typical scene of a gathering on the steps of the church of San Pedro.

Resbalosa street going down towards the Plaza de Armas.

Two corners of Cuzco: the
Santa Clara arch and the
surroundings of the church
of San Pedro.

The streets of Cuzco are
steep and winding.

The fortress of Sacsayhuaman is defended by three parallel walls.

On June 24th the Inca festivity of Inti-Raymi is celebrated on the esplanade of Sacsayhuaman. This ceremony was dedicated to the sun.

beliefs in the popular festivities. The religious calender of Peru coincides with the pagan one, with the old solar cycles of agriculture. Old native traditions emerge from the outer wrapping of Roman Catholic ceremonies. In Ayacucho the **Nazarene** of Julcamarca is worshipped, whose beard actually grows. In Huaraz they pray to the Lord of la Soledad who broke a rock to emerge with his cross. In Sapallanga they worship the Virgin of the Stone who appeared like the river nymphs in the waters of a spring.

The most important and popular folk festivity is celebrated every year on june 24th on the esplanade at Sacsayhuamán.

This ceremony is to replace the famous Festival of the Sun (Inti Raymi) which took place at the time of the Incas in the main square of Cuzco. Today, folk groups enact all the ritual of Inti Raymi in the fortress of Sacsayhuamán with the arrival of the Inca king, the salutation of the sun, canticles, dances and rogations.

Among the patently indigenous ceremonies, those of special interest are the wrestling contests of Tocto and Chiaraje, in which men challenge one another to fight and gain the attention of the women, and the pilgrimage of the indians dressed up as bears to the summit of Coyllur Riti. While the faithful worship Our Lord Jesus Christ, the indians dance on the mountains and on the glaciers in homage to the Sun god. This same merging of traditions is to be found in the popular dances. Some Spanish dances are still preserved from the colonial period: minuettes, courtly dances, masquerades of Moors and Christians... Among the Spanish celebrations most deeply rooted in the Peruvian soul is without any doubt Holy Week. In many cities throughout the country such as Arequipa and Ayacucho, there is great religious fervour and local colour.

There is an enormous variety of popular costumes. Almost everyone uses the poncho. And some, like those from the region of Cuzco, show a pronounced Spanish influence. The women's dress is of many colours and generally topped by an amusing hat whose decoration changes according to whether the wearer is single, widowed, or married.

In Lima there is still a fondness for cock-fighting, an

Heralds with music announce the arrival of the Inca at the festivities of the sun.

activity which enjoyed great popularity among the Spaniards. But most of all, the capital has a great bull-fighting tradition. The people of Lima are proud of having the oldest bull ring in the world, built in the year 1766.

In many places throughout the country carnivals are celebrated in homage to the fecund forces of nature. These festivities are at their most brilliant in the region of lake Titicaca.

The great musical sense of the Indian is evident in all Peruvian folklore. The flute, (la quena) made of cane or bone, is the most characteristic national instrument, and is normally accompanied by the drum and the harp.

Young girls dressed as Inca virgins at the Inti-Raymi festivities.

THE PERUVIAN

The Peruvian is biologically the product of a mixture of races, and spiritually the heir to a variety of cultures. Spanish characteristics and those of African and Asian stock being added to the primitive indigenous elements. Nowadays, it is generally accepted that the first inhabitants of Peru reached the Andes from the continent of Asia. And it is to these nomadic people that the ancient cultures of the Sierra Norteña and lake Titicaca must be attributed.

The mixture of the primitive tribes and the Incas was enriched by the introduction of Spanish blood after the conquest. The Crown itself patronized this fusion

Warlike dances at the Inti-Raymi festivities.

of the races in both social and legal spheres. The Peruvian indian is strong and of average height. He is extremely resistent to heights and to walking long distances, living according to a simple moral code: ama sua, ama llulla, ama kella — do not steal, do not lie, do not be idle.

This variety of race has fortunately produced a great richness of character. Viceregal history has influenced the Spanish-indian (cholo) of the mountains. The Inca culture has left its mark on the people of the interior. The supersticious and poetical past of the Aymaras still lives in the inhabitants of the puna.

THE RUINS AT CHAN-CHAN AND MACHU PICCHU

Peruvian archaeology is extraordinarily rich. In every corner of the country there are scattered remains of ancient cultures. Ruins, necropolises, and museums bear witness to the original civilizations of the country. From Cajamarca to Ica we come upon remains of the Chavín culture which developed eight centuries before the Christian era. In the region of Paracas, around the I century, a civilization flourished which was distinguished by the richness of its fabrics. And from the III and IV centuries the

A general view of Pisac and the Vilcanota valley.

expansion of the Mochica and Nazca cultures took place with their magnificent hydraulic engineering feats in the arid zone of Peru.

All these cultures either disappeared prematurely or fell under the advance of the Incas in the middle of the XV century. Only the Chimú culture, which had developed in the north on the foundation of the Mochica civilization, offered any resistence to the expanding Inca empire. The ruins of Chan-Chan, the capital of the Chimú kingdom can still give a remote idea of what that immense sun-dried brick city must have been like. Legend speaks of famous treasure taken by the Spanish conquerors from the mud of

Chan-Chan. Seekers of jewels have contributed more effectively than the passing of time to the destruction of the city. In spite of all this, the appearance of the ruins is still an impressive one with warehouses, barns, irrigation channels, dams, dwellings and sun-dried brick hills; also two protective walls several kilometres in length.

The expansion of the Inca empire was to put an end to the splendour of these primitive cultures. The Inca organization began to develop in the environs of Cuzco until it succeeded in creating, at the time of Pachacutec in the XV century, an extensive empire 5000 kilometres in length. Along the famous Inca highways, where the chasquis, or postal service ran, many remains can still be found of this severe civilization based on a strict social organization. But the great Inca sanctuary, excelling in its grandeur all the ruins of the empire, from Ollantaytambo to Sacsayhuamán, rises up like a condor's nest above the granite canyon of Urubamba, in the first outposts of the jungle. Machu Picchu is a city built close to the sky, surrounded by walls more than a metre thick. It is a fortress inhabited by spirits and magical silences, like the very cosmic universe where the sun revolves. Inside its perimeter, the sun, moon, clouds and stars were worshipped. Only legend dares to explain the sacred origin of this aerial city. Tradition says that the Qoriq'ente, the golden bird that sings in

A flock of llamas on the plateau.

Different views of the market at Pisac where, as in ancient times, barter is still practised.

paradise, gave man the secret of changing stones into mud. Another legend tells that a god made men into stone so that the Incas would drag them, going through severe punishment along the way, to the top of Machu Picchu. The ruins of the sacred city retain the magic of their past history; their life wasted away gradually like the lament of the imperial maidens who were present at the twilight of the Inca empire and the death of the children of the Sun. But history still flows, like a lament, along the pathways it has cut. The discovery of Machu Picchu was made by Hiram Bingham who found the ruins in July 1911.

All trace of the sacred city had been lost since the XVI century, when Tupac Amaru was executed by the Viceroy Francisco de Toledo.

Neither is it known with any degree of certainty when the city was built. By the design of its architecture, it could date from the time of King Pachacutec, who reigned in the middle of the XV century. One of its principal attractions is in the mystery of its origin and the secret nature of its history. The imagination of the traveller must find an answer to all these questions. It is sufficient to scan the peak of Huayna Picchu, where the planets reposed, or to gaze upon the darkness of the imperial tomb inhabited by death, or to listen to the whistling of the wind as it blows over the sentry boxes where the imperial soldiers stood guard, or to stay for a while beside the altars to the Sun...

The small Cuzco-Santa Ana railway leading to Machu-Picchu.

The Hiram Bingham roadway, built in 1948 winds upwards to the Machu-Picchu Tourist Hotel.

A general view of the ruins of Machu-Picchu.

A partial view of the ruins of Machu-Picchu.

To the south of the Plaza Sagrada is the Priest's House.

Several views of Inca houses and buildings.

Inca buildings at Machu-Picchu: the Sala de los Morteros, the Temple of the three windows, the Royal Mausoleum and the Temple of the Sun.

The Plaza Sagrada.

Sacrificial altars and the entrance to the torture chamber. Lower down on the right is the famous Intihuatana or "place where the sun is fixed". Some researchers believe that this stone was used for studying the movements of the sun and moon.

Alpacas and llamas, animals characteristic of the Peruvian fauna.

The Amarus or Serpents pass looks out onto the
impressive silhouette of Huayna-Picchu (young hill).

The ancient Incas cultivated these lands cutting terraces out of the mountain side.

LAKE TITICACA

Situated at more than 3,800 metres above sea level, Titicaca is the highest navigable lake on our planet. On its banks stretches a rich agricultural and cattle-breeding area: el Collao. The inhabitants of el Collao are Quechuas or Aymaras. But near to Puno, the last Peruvian town on the frontier with Bolivia, the last representatives of the tribe of the Uro indians can still be found.

The Uros are descendents of the original inhabitants of the lake. They are such a primitive race that they considered themselves subhuman, and were convinced that they had black blood and because of this, could never either feel the cold, or die from drowning; they were the idle kings of Titicaca, the proud and miserable lords of the lake. They certainly caused a problem for the strict labour organization of the

Inca track and bridge carved over the canyon, on the way to Huayna Picchu.

Inca empire, which did not allow inactivity on the part of any of its subjects. The Jesuit Oliva, in the XVI century, tells of an original solution thought out by the administration of the empire to occupy these lazy subjects in some task. They were obliged to hand over a cane full of fleas every month. The Uro, mixed with the Aymaras, live today in the Bahía de Chucuito, on floating islands built with cane or reed-mace. They live of their fishing, and sail over the blue waters of the lake in their golden boats as they did hundreds of years ago. The best archaeological monuments of the Collao of Peru date from different times; there are las chullpas (pre-Inca graves), and the colonial churches erected by the Spanish missionaries.

Some of these churches, dating from the XVI, XVII, and XVIII centuries can be visited in the old mission centre of Juli.

The lake Titicaca region is of exceptional human interest as it has jealously guarded the characteris-

The Sacred Valley of the Incas

tics of native life there. The Aymara indians who inhabit el Collao were probably the creators of the Tiahuanaco culture which spread throughout Peru from the IX century, before the development of the Inca empire. These are people who are adapted to the altitude and to the difficulties of life on the plateau. They maintain their rich folk tradition based on old warlike and religious customs. The "diablada", symbolizing the struggle between good and evil is one of the most characteristic dances in the region. It is probably very primitive in origin and as remote as the animistic religion of the people of the plateau; but with the arrival of the Spanish missionaries, some Catholic influences began to be felt. The majority of the Titicaca indians were shepherds, a less strenuous occupation than tilling the earth in those high areas wasted by erosion.

THE OASIS OF AREQUIPA

The oasis of Arequipa lies in a peaceful slumber between the volcanoes and the sea. It is bathed by the waters of the river Chili, and the cristalline freshness of its springs, which have, according to the peasants, healing properties, at el Pozo Negro, la Media

An aerial shot of the Andes.

The village of Ollantaytambo, two thousand seven hundred metres high.

Lake Titicaca at the height of Puno.

The ruins of the Inca fortress of Ollantaytambo

Craftsmen from Puno weaving.

Luna, Catari and los Ojos de Characato etc. In the midst of this pleasant luminous countryside rise the snow-capped peaks of the volcanoes Misti, Chachani and Pichu Pichu. Cervantes wrote of the eternal springtime at Arequipa. Other authors, inspired by the clearness of its skies, have described the delicate outline of the countryside where the gold of the corn mingles with the green of the alfalfa grass, and the silver thread of the canals with the feminine melancholy of the willows. Arequipa, the capital of the region, is a white city with a clean appearance. Built with the porous rock of volcanoes it is like the top of one, covered with a frosted whiteness. It bears pronounced traces of its colonial past. Some parts are reminiscent of the white villages of

The island of the Uro indians on Lake Titicaca.

Uro indians sitting at the door of a reed hut.

Andalusia, perhaps because these southern lands of Peru, so familiar with the old cultures, received the sharp buffet of the western mode and imperial officiousness with a certain Andalusian scepticism. With their leisurely rhythm, these old villages test any innovation with the repose of a siesta, and in the calm of a quiet courtyard.

The colonial culture, however, has left in Arequipa some of its finest monuments: the neoclassical façade of the cathedral and its treasure, the churches of La Merced and San Francisco, the church of the Company. Not forgetting the Monastery of Saint Catherine, which encloses within its walls all the mystery and gracefulness of the XVI architecture of Arequipa. The Monastery of Saint Catherine was closed to visitors until 1970. The silence of its cloisters

has converted it, through the centuries, into a dwelling place of peace, inhabited like a heart in love, by a source of life of its own and the bitter oranges of loneliness. The monastery is like a town in miniature. Its streets and squares all have Spanish names: Toledo, Granada, Málaga, Burgos, Seville... It could be said that Santa Catalina is a Spanish village painted red and indigo by the imagination of an indian. The old colonial mansions doubtless constitute another of the charms of Arequipa. In one of them, —la Fundación El Fierro—, the City Museum has been established. Others, such as the houses of Moral, Yriberry, Rickets, Goyeneche and de la Moneda, are among the most noteworthy examples of Peruvian architecture.

Next to these historic relics of former times, a modern city is developing, living of its industry and tourist trade. And in the outskirts, close to the "young villages", new residential colonies are being set up spreading along the picturesque valley where the thermal springs are born.

Spanish tradition is naturally deep-rooted in the calender of festivities in Arequipa, ranging from the Holy Week celebrations to pilgrimages and excursions to the sanctuaries. And on the great peasant feast days there is the brave spectacle of the bull-fight.

The Santa Catalina Museum houses a valuable collection of religious art comprising several works from the Cuzco school of painting, some pictures by Spanish and Italian masters, carvings, and other original objects of colonial art.

THE SCENERY

The land of Peru is rich and varied in contrasts. From the sandy soil of the desert to the luxuriant vegetation of the jungle; the wide plains where the llama grazes, to the wild mountain ranges. There are three major regions: the coast, the mountain area, and the jungle. The coastal region is dry and desert-like and stretches between the Andes and the sea; it has been transformed into one of the richest areas in Peru. The dams and irrigation systems favour the cultivation of sugar and cotton. Great fishing factories utilize the fruits of the sea. Numerous marine species, from great cetaceans to tiny anchovies feed on the plankton brought by the cold waters of the Peruvian or Humboldt current. Birds also feed on the anchovy; pelicans, seagulls and guanayes snatch it from the surface on the sea. From the droppings of the guanayes a fine fertilizer is obtained which the natives call «guano».

The Sierra, or mountainous region, constitutes 26% of the country and holds half the population. Its altitude demands inhabitants with "a large heart"; but, on the other hand, it offers clear luminous skies, picturesque villages surrounded by tiny fields, and Franciscan orchards. This land where the potato was first grown, is fertile, but beyond a height of

A Uro village in the marshy area of the bay of Chucuito. The indians conserve many of their ancestral customs.

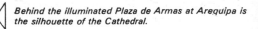 *Behind the illuminated Plaza de Armas at Arequipa is the silhouette of the Cathedral.*

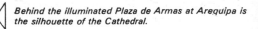 *A view of the façade and organ of Arequipa Cathedral.*

The little square of San Francisco has the peaceful charm of the old corners of Arequipa.

The Sabandia windmill; a fine example of the architecture of the Arequipa region.

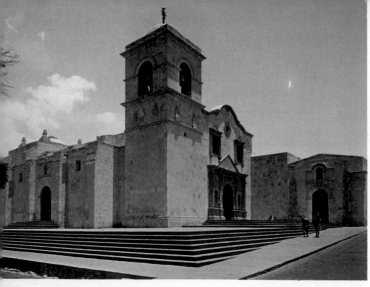

Façade and cloister of the church of San Francisco with mozarabic influences in its roof and archways.

The Plaza de Armas at Arequipa where the city was
founded. All its north side is occupied by the elegant
neoclassical façade of the Cathedral.

Façade of the Monastery of Santa Catalina.

Granada Street, wide and sunny, comes out under the dome of
the church of Santa Catalina.

3,500 metres begins the frozen plain — la puna. There, llamas, alpacas, and vicuñas graze amid the stormy winds, the lonely heights, and the wild straw plains. Only the lakes soften the puna scenery. On the shores of lake Titicaca, according to the legend, God created the first inhabitants of Peru: Manco Cápac and Mamma Ocllo. The jungle, on the eastern slopes of the Andes, is the most extensive region in Peru, but also the least populated. The new communication networks have already penetrated into these sultry hidden lands, forbidden to the ancient Incas. An inaccessible, untrodden land, the Inca Garcilaso called it. The land becomes even more inaccessible and less trodden as we penetrate into the jungle. Amazonian earth with vague waters and immense floods where the villages of the interior seem to sleep in a mysterious, almost vegetal state.

The stone fountain playing in the Plaza Zocodover.

The future of the country is probably hidden under this disguise of cedar, rubber, mahogany, and green leaves. Civilization has already reached the shores of the great rivers (the Marañón, the Ucayali, and the Amazon), and even the very settlements built by the Spanish missionaries. Peru is a true geographical compendium, with the desert, the tundra, the Andes, and the tropical jungle... It is easily understood why its primaeval inhabitants lacked the inclination to imagine other lands beyond the sea. It seems impossible for there to exist another world beyond the horizon, where the fiery condor sinks every evening at the solemn and magic hour of dusk.

IQUITOS AND THE JUNGLE

The three most outstanding features in the geography of Peru are of course, the sea, the Andes,

One of the courtyards in Santa Catalina.

The façade of the Monastery's art gallery.

and the Amazon river. It is the water of the mighty Amazon and its tributaries that irrigates the green jungle area. Several groups of aborigines speaking different languages live scattered in the magical vegetable world of this region. Yucca constitutes the staple food for the majority of its inhabitants; this is eaten boiled or mixed with other foods.

Iquitos is the most important town in the east of Peru, in the heart of the jungle. Formerly an abandoned Jesuit mission, it began to grow in 1864 when the river posting place of Loreto was established. From the end of the XIX century to the beginning of this, it was the centre for the rich rubber trade. Great mansions bear witness to a past splendour which ended in 1912 with the ruin of the rubber trade. Its social club, built at the time of the great fortunes, comes from the Paris international exhibition of 1889, where it was bought by a rubber millionaire, who had it taken to the jungle. Iquitos is today the capital of the Amazon. Its avenues dip into the left bank of that great river. Orchids, giant trees, and fabulous birds give it a magic atmosphere and a tender, humid tone. The murmur of the jungle penetrates its streets; the fleshy fruits of paradise —the cocona, the guayaba, the naranjilla, and the

The interior of the art gallery which houses a notable collection of colonial style paintings.

The choir in the church of Santa Catalina.

Wake or «De profundis» room.

maracuyá — flood its markets; the mystery of the Amazon reaches the floating houses of the Port of Belén, reminiscent of the river cities of Bangkok and Hong Kong. The tiles on the outside of its buildings give the town a characteristic air. Iquitos is an excellent starting point for journeys into the jungle. A few hours sail up river finds one in a settlement of the Yagua indians or on the white sandy beaches of the river Momón. The Omagua and Cocama indians live on the shores of the river Itaya, a tributary of the Amazon.

Those fond of hunting can organize safaris in the ebb-tide season, from June to December. The fishermen, however, go to the lakes. In these waters there are many paiches, an enormous fish eaten by the natives in salted fillets dried in the sun.

The jungle folklore has an abundance of imagination and superstition and a rich oral tradition including fine stories and legends. The indians in the region make interesting hand-made objects: bows and arrows, blow-pipes and fans...

The Misti volcano, its mass overlooking the Arequipa region.

Yagua indians from the jungle.

The Amazon Lodge, a tourist hotel in the Iquitos jungle.

The Jibaro indians go hunting armed with their long blow-pipes.

A warrior of the Yagua tribe who lives on the shores on the Amazon.

The Amazon flows through the dense vegetation of the jungle.

The mighty Amazon, near Iquitos.

Twilight on the waters of the Amazon near Iquitos.

Index

Printed in Spain   GEOCOLOR®
M.R-T.M